Equine Angels

A wandering foal looks for Mom in the mist.

Equine Angels

Stories of Rescue, Love, and Hope

Frank Weller

Photographs by Donna M. Cloutier

The Lyons Press
Guilford, Connecticut

An imprint of The Globe Pequot Press

This book is dedicated to all those who rescue equines, humans, or any of God's creatures. It is your dedication and passion that inspire us and many others, especially in the most difficult times. You remind us that in rescuing and healing, we, too, are rescued and healed. What you give becomes its own reward and the graceful example of your giving inspires many to get involved. May God bless you all!

Ubi Caritas, Deus ibi est!
When love is in the heart, God is there!

To buy books in quantity for corporate use or incentives, call **(800) 962–0973** or e-mail **premiums@GlobePequot.com.**

The Lyons Press is an imprint of The Globe Pequot Press

Text design by Sheryl P. Kober
Layout by Melissa Evarts
Unless otherwise noted, all photographs are by Donna M. Cloutier

Library of Congress Cataloging-in-Publication Data is available on file.

ISBN 978-1-59921-444-3

Printed in China

10 9 8 7 6 5 4 3 2 1

A moment in the mist.

CONTENTS

The Belgians shake the ground in pregnant passage.

Mares and a foal.

Being with the Angels

Frank Weller

Is it time to get up?

Being with the Angels is a joy that comforts me
Being with the Angels is sweet serenity

Being with the Angels is like a foal's warm soft breath
Being with the Angels gives me great happiness

Being with the Angels is where I hope to be
Being with the Angels trotting to eternity

Being with the Equine Angels lifts my soul, God, up to thee
Being with the Angels where the rescues rescue me

PREFACE

Just like human children, equine children often raise us and rescue us. They challenge us and rejuvenate us, while all the time teaching us. Horses, in general, can accompany us and guide us as insightful partners on our path through life. We are blessed to have them and I've always considered it an honor and privilege to work with or for them, because horses are intuitively inspiring as companions and teachers.

Before rescue, my passion was documentary film. I started combining my love of horses and film by doing a profile of a horse rescuer named Helen Meredith. I followed her to Canada as she worked to find new homes for Premarin foals that she had bought at auction—foals that are the by-product of the drug industry's need for pregnant mare urine, or PMU.

PMU has been used to create human hormone replacement therapy medications for more than sixty years. The term can apply to the mares, the foals, or the farms on which they are bred. The multibillion-dollar enterprise requires a harsh collection process, in which the mares must stand in stanchions, hooked up to collection apparatus, unable to turn or lie down, from the fourth to the eleventh months of their pregnancies. Bladder infections and lameness can occur. The mares are also deprived of lateral recumbency, or lying-down sleep, which horses need. In most cases, the foals born to the pregnant mares are considered disposable by-products of manufacturing the drug. In past years, the foals that were auctioned for slaughter each year numbered in the tens of thousands, and by many accounts more than fifty thousand were at risk every year. Recently, as the use of hormone replacement therapy drugs has declined, the mares have been taken out of service and also sold for slaughter.

1

The auction houses were sad places where nervous foals that had been separated, but not weaned, from their moms were gathered in several large pens. The foals were herded into a series of chutes that eventually led to the auction pit. They entered the pit in groups or lots to be bid upon. Scared and sniffing the air, looking for moms to save them, they scrambled around the auction pit in front of a large audience. Reminiscent of the Roman Coliseum, the audience, mostly made up of "killer buyers" working for meat packers, was indifferent to their pain and panic. The successful bidder would then have the lot of foals herded to his holding pen through another series of chutes that led from the auction pit.

Helen, who was doing three jobs at once, needed help. I can't remember if she ever asked, but I found myself feeding, herding, gentling, and helping her process the foals for shipping to the United States. I would pick up the camera occasionally to chronicle our progress or for a quick interview, but mostly I was working with the foals—160 of them to be exact. The energy was amazing; it was very invigorating. The foals were timid, curious, nervous, and herd oriented, sometimes behaving like a school of fish, but they always had incredible energy. For me, it was literally a fountain of youth! Watching them during the rare break was mesmerizing, like watching a crackling fire, or your first two-year-old child at play. They were fascinating and entertaining, and you couldn't help but think of where their future would take them.

I'm not sure when I actually crossed the line from observer/documentarian to horse rescuer, but I do believe that each vocation has helped me perform better in the other. Good observation is very important when assessing, learning from, or teaching horses—and people, too, for that matter. Skillful horse rescue requires being a good observer and also demands that you find good homes for the rescued horses, usually by telling their stories. Horse rescuing has strengthened the observer and documentary film-

maker in me, but as you will see, that is just the beginning. It only took one season of auctions for us to go running in search of a better way to rescue foals. One that did not involved the disease-ridden, terrifying auction experience.

A foal keeps an eye on his mom.

I started Equine Angels Rescue Sanctuary (EARS) as a way to help the foals find loving forever homes. Operating as a 501(c)3 charity, EARS makes it easier to recruit the village it takes to save a horse, and to beg for the donations that are also imperative. We need volunteers because

3

Covering all angles for protection.

The soul of the mare is beautiful.

the task is overwhelming, and because no one should have that much fun alone. It is also rewarding to stay in touch with the adopting families and monitor their progress, leading to more fun and inspiring stories. I followed the first group of foals to their eventual everlasting families, and it has become part of our mission to keep in touch. We want to know that horse and family are doing well, and frequently we happily provide some assistance or wisdom.

The mares and foals move as one.

Horses necking.

Standing next to Mom is the safest place to be.

The year after first becoming involved with the foals, I met the mares. The mares, especially, evoke a primal grace as they patiently wait for new life or shepherd the youngsters at their sides. You can see the mares' instinctive dedication to motherhood just by watching their devotion and determination in walking, grazing, and upon birth, guarding and nursing their young. At first, newborns are little shadows, glued to a small orbit around Mom, but gradually they become bold and, like teenagers, ever more curious about their rugged environment. We can see the foals learning from their moms in this age-old chain of nurturing and mothering.

The human participants of EARS could not sit idly by while these

magnificent horses were killed. If it was just a matter of those lives saved, that would have been enough, but fortunately, we have come to know the greater potential of these angelic equines. Each of the horses from EARS has touched and uplifted several human lives along the rescue path. The rescuers, the volunteers, the donors, the foster families, and people who just care, all get a feeling of peace, joy, and love as they connect with and save these beautiful animals. The lives of the eventual adopting families are also enhanced when bonding with these noble souls.

Mom is always the best guardian.

Personally, when I get lost at any particular point on my journey, I visit the horses and let them quietly come to me. Somehow, they give me strength and guidance to get me through a day or even just a minute of a

Two colts looking for adventure.

complicated life. Like angels, the horses reassure me. Being with them has a centering effect on me, and during my time with them my thoughts settle and I find clarity about the next step I should take. Knowing that my hands have guided and gentled many foals and mares on the way to their new loving homes, I can accept and absorb this same form of comfort from them as well. I have often thought that when one of us who has loved and worked with these wondrous spirits passes on, there might be a happy, healthy herd of horses to guide us and gentle us through the final part of our journey home. The volunteers of EARS have learned along the way that "rescues rescue us" and, indeed, we also derive an abundance of peace, joy, and love as we help these kindred spirits.

In so many small steps I've learned about life and wisdom through watching and working with the mares and foals I've helped to rescue over the years. They teach patience, sensibility, problem solving, family raising, focus, and friendship. The catch, however, is that you must be open to the lesson, watching, waiting, and wondering how even the smallest movement of a tail or an ear might mean so much. This is where the subtle becomes spiritual, and that is another secret that they share. Baby steps mean a lot. Mothers, of course, are the best teachers.

These mares and foals have a connection with the world that is mysterious and mystical. In my life, they are a portal to the creator and a link to the infinite. I have found possibility and purpose by looking deeply into their eyes. Horses can raise us up physically, mentally, and spiritually beyond our innate limits. They are a gift for which we should be thankful.

The EARS rescue team hopes that you will also share the mares' and foals' stories with someone you know—someone who should know about their fate—and we thank you in advance. People have often asked me if the "Equine Angels" are the humans who save the horses or the horses who save the humans. I believe that the answer lives within this book. Herein are the stories and images that illustrate how that happens. Enjoy your own journey along the rescue path.

For the horses,
Frank Weller, founder of EARS

The herd has found water.

Rescue

The foal is in a small orbit around his mom.

The Spring of Equine Creation

FRANK WELLER

The mist, the gray, floating mist, it surrounded us. We could only sense the vast size of the wet silvery cloud that we were standing in. It was still mid-spring but very chilly, because this was the province of Manitoba in Canada. In the distance there was a faint beating sound, but we saw nothing. The muffled reverberation gave no clue as to the direction of its origin. We waited inside the hollow of the cloud as the sound grew slightly louder. There was a clearing for about a hundred yards, but the mist shrouded the far side like a gigantic silver curtain. It was almost noon and the mist was very bright as the ground began to shake while the rhythmic beating became louder yet. Suddenly, across the clearing, the curtain was broken by a wall of blurry figures that were obviously moving toward us with great power, speed, and the churning sound of a train. When the wall was about fifty feet away, everything stopped. The clattering noise, the blurry figures, the vibrations coming up our legs, all stopped. Reality went to freeze-frame. When we focused our eyes, we could see that the wall was actually made of horses. Mares in many colors and combinations of colors stood along with newly born foals attached to some of them, echoing their colors or contrasting them. They were looking us over with eyes as wide as ours watching them. It would have been silent except for the snorts and long breaths of the horses. The only pounding we felt then was that of our own hearts.

The herd sometimes moves in unison, like a school of fish or soldiers marching to the same beat.

"Pepper," the stallion, leads the herd to better pasture.

There was one horse in front, leading the herd. He was a huge and powerful black and white stallion. We believed that he was the one they called Pepper. On his cue, the wall slowly walked toward us, the aliens they had encountered. Frozen with awe, we rapidly remembered that we should be documenting this dreamlike contact that seemed as though it was happening in a prehistoric time. The mares were beautiful, big and beautiful. Some who had not yet

The foal learns about his legs.

21

Two colts keep a
constant eye on
Mom.

had their foals were bus-like in size, but somehow still elegant as they boldly walked up to inspect us. It was a wonder to us that they could walk, much less run. Many were curious about us as they approached, and others seemed protective, especially if a foal was nestled next to them. The babies were also curious but took frequent cues from their moms, who seemed to hold a short invisible leash on them. After coming within ten feet and looking us over for a

A mother's love.

A band of mares with new foals gathers on the plains of Canada.

Starting life close to Mom.

few moments, the stallion pawed the ground and gave a grunt, signaling a retreat. Surprisingly, the lead mare, standing next to him, countered his command. She wanted to stay a bit and pawed back at him and squealed as if to say, "In just a minute." He demurred and the wall of horses stood looking at us for at least another fifteen seconds until the stallion slightly reared and more forcibly said, "Okay, let's go!" in no uncertain terms. He turned them all around and before they disappeared back into the mist, we saw some of the foals playfully kicking up their heels and looking like jumping beans as they frolicked and ran away.

In the mist, it almost seemed as though we were in the womb with the babies. It was wet, murky, and silent as we encountered many other bands of mares. Some bands had stallions to rebreed the mares, and some did not. We witnessed the social interactions and the stallions' different styles of herding the mares. Loo, a magnificent paint stallion, would let his mares range widely, while Pepper kept his band of mares in a close group. We felt honored and humbled to observe their lives and the beginnings of new life. It was hallowed ground and we were privileged to be on those wide open Canadian plains that were like an equine cathedral. We could not contain our sense of wonder, gratitude, and joy. Indeed, this was a sacred eternal spring that poured forth the lives of thousands of foals mothered by the regal mares.

Innovative Rescue—A Better Way

FRANK WELLER

After witnessing group after group of horses put through the auction pit, I could hardly stand it. Even frequent breaks didn't make the auction experience tolerable. As Helen Meredith, founder of United Pegasus, exclaimed, "It's the ones that are left behind that you are worried about." How do you sit there and watch wave after wave of beautiful baby horses and stately mares go to feedlot operators and killer buyers?

The foals are born throughout the month of May. The mares are bred again as the stallions are released into the fields during their first breeding heat in June. The auctions for the foals start in early September, and at that time the foals and their moms are separated. It would normally be too early to wean a foal humanely, much less callously separate mare and foal, never to be together again. Many important stages of mental and physical development are crushed or stunted. The antibodies in the mothers' milk are important in protecting youngsters from disease. Their new diet frequently becomes hay, to which rolled oats are sometimes added—a very bad developmental choice. These foals are often seen trying to nurse from other foals, and it is a pitiful sight.

Equine Angels Rescue Sanctuary (EARS) could only take fifty foals that first year. How do you decide which ones, especially when many of them are in a state of panic? The situation is complicated by the fact

Foals are curious creatures.

Constrained and confused. COLIN CORNEAU, COURTESY OF THE *VANCOUVER SUN*

that these auctions can be breeding grounds for disease. Also, the babies are terrified by the process of being separated, not properly weaned, from their mothers, in many cases at only three months of age.

As we approached our second year of rescue we knew we had to do better. We reached out to several PMU farmers whom we had met at the auctions and endeavored to work with them for a win-win-win outcome. Some of them were enthusiastic about helping us to help them and the horses, and some of them wouldn't even consider it. We had learned that

Love bites.

The numbers on their foreheads identify these foals for border crossing.

the rebred mares don't go into the collection barns until early November because until their fourth month of pregnancy, there is not enough estrogen in their urine to bother collecting it. The mares must go into the barns "dry," which means not lactating. If the foals are not with them for two weeks, they stop lactating.

The farmers allowed us to go to the farms in August and select groups of foals that would stay with their moms until mid-October. By paying the farmer the prevailing prices directly, we were able to prevent the foals from going to auction, and kept the mares and foals together an extra six weeks. The foals avoided the terror and germs of the auction house, the

farmer didn't have to spend the time and effort moving the foals to market, the foals spent another one-third of their young lives with their mothers, and the eventual adopting families got a more established equine that was better off mentally and physically.

It was also easier to "read" more about the suitable adoption characteristics of the foals when they were out in the field with Mom and not in a stressful situation. Those traits include conformation, breed, psychological balance, sociability, and gender. With this additional knowledge, we could try to pre-match requested horses for speedier adoption, determine which horses might make better adoption candidates, and rescue a balanced

Rescued tails.

As heavy as they are, the mares are surprisingly swift.

The mares are ever vigilant.

group of breed, temperament, gender, and color to provide a better range of choice for adopters. Rescuers were less stressed as well, which meant that with this approach we encountered less burnout.

We realized that many stories of difficulties with PMU foals were the result of the problems presented by the old way of marketing the foals through auctions. Some rescue groups ended up with sick horses because of the communal auction experience. On top of all the good work they were trying to do, they would end up maintaining and medicating foals, which was a costly postponement of a successful adoption. Sometimes the foals

would be hard to gentle or be more resistant to human contact because of the early separation from their mothers, or because their only interaction with humans at an early age was negative.

"Joker" was one of the first rescued foals.

The foals go out in groups to explore.

It seems that the best change we ever made in the rescue process was to work with the farmers.

Now, our rescued foals have the chance to be much better established. They are nurtured physically and psychologically by Mom for as long as possible—an extra six weeks of their young lives. Their behavior is more balanced, they are easier to train, and they are better candidates for adoption. The foals also more easily endure the thirty-six-hour ride from Canada and have a faster recovery time from that trip. The contrast is remarkable.

Another benefit of working with the farmers is that, although we didn't agree with their choices, we developed a dialogue with them for the betterment of the horses. At times, we were able to successfully suggest some dietary changes and handling protocols that improved the condition of the mares and foals.

Maybe the greater moral is that if people who might be at odds (such as PMU farmer and rescuer) work together, then the world can be a far better place for all.

A new foal stays close to Mom but is very curious.

Finding New Life

NICOLE CLOUTIER

My mother and I drove down the muddy roads of Ashern, Manitoba, in our little rental car. The road was straight and riddled with potholes, just like all the other roads in the town, due to the heavy rain that every local joked we had brought with us. This, our last day on the farms, was the first day we weren't wearing our bright blue rain suits and woolen hats, even though it was May. We were headed toward the field of what had become our favorite herd, a group of Percheron mares and their newly born foals. Perhaps it was just because there was no stud, but this particular group had become used to us walking around their field with all our heavy camera equipment. Most of the horses simply ignored us, only glancing up as we passed. Others loved our attention, rubbing their faces on our backs or nibbling our hair. I had grown particularly attached to one white, still-pregnant mare I had named Eden. The first evening we spent with her herd I stood with her, scratching her forelock and shoulders. If I walked away, she would follow and then stand over me, her neck resting on my shoulder as I took photos of the other horses. I told her that I would be back in the morning, if only she could hold on a bit longer. My mother and I had yet to see a birth.

43

Nicole meets a
pregnant mare.

Our first day, we had walked out into the field of a band led by a black and white stallion the farmers had named Pepper. At this point we weren't really sure what to expect, so when the entire herd came charging toward us, Pepper in the lead, we did what any sane photographer would do: we pulled out our cameras.

Luckily, the horses showed no intention of running us over. They paused about five small steps in front of us, flared their nostrils, grunted, then turned and ran off. We just stood there watching them disappear, prac-

tically in step with one another as if it had been rehearsed. My heart threatened to break through my ribs. I knew these horses weren't wild in the truest sense of the word, but even I, someone who had been completely aware of their purpose and lives for the past four years, believed I was looking wilderness in the face. Seeing these mares in their natural environment made me almost forget the seven months of their eleven month pregnancy that they spent immobilized, while their urine was collected. The summer became

Nicole checks the condition of a pregnant mare near delivery.

The stallions of two bands approach each other to . . .

. . . discuss their territories and . . .

. . . then depart to their own herds.

Moms make the
best teachers . . .

their season, when even they could believe they were as wild as their cousins in the southwestern United States.

The herd came back to check us out a few more times before they calmed down and seemed to forget we were even there at all. Then, they went back to what I imagine was their normal behavior. Mothers grazing, reaching over every few minutes to brush their sleeping foals with their noses. Younger foals stayed in perfect step with their mothers, legs lifting high over tall grass, while older ones strayed farther

away, leaping over the grass like they were mere pebbles. One black and white colt reared, tossing his front legs as high in the air as he could reach. The muscles in his neck and legs were lean and wet with the sweat he had built up. The sight reminded me of the stallion he could have become if this had been, in fact, the wild. He might even have been in charge of his own herd like his father before him, protecting it from wandering humans. He came down on the back of a younger foal, whose mother promptly chased the black and white

. . . and the foals had better be good students.

Moms tell their children the wisdom of the ages.

away. Meanwhile, his own mother grazed on grass and early morning dew, seemingly nonchalant even when the colt stuck his nose under her hips for his breakfast, and I remembered how young he was.

As the herd became more trusting of us, I could also see a change in our own behaviors. Over the day, my three teammates and I had spread out across the field. From my station I could see them all strategically posed, cameras set on their tripods, waiting for the herd to come to them. I don't know what caused the herd to startle, but I had seen it happen before and I did what felt right—I dropped to my knees and waited. I still believe it was this show of trust, or subjection, that made them pause in front of me, foals standing warily

The window of new life.

New legs don't always work on the first try and tire easily . . .

. . . until Mom thinks it's time to try again.

Mutual affection.

behind their mothers on wobbly legs. One palomino filly, that had been born just earlier that morning, peeked out from behind her mother, who reached out her neck and nudged my head. If I had stretched out my arm then, I could have touched the filly's nose, but I didn't dare. Instead, I held my breath, not wanting to make any movement that would scare them away. Getting a picture was the last thing on my mind.

The Percherons were easier. Most of the mares there were still pregnant. This was another reason we had chosen to return to them on our last day;

The mares confer on a scent.

The Belgian mares eating for six.

they presented the highest likelihood of showing us a birth. Also, with their foals still tucked safely inside their bellies, they showed no fear, following us around the field, rubbing their heads on our backs, and almost knocking over our tripods when we weren't looking. It was here I had met Eden.

She looked a bit older than some of the other mares, her heavy belly reaching toward the ground rather than out to the sides. While there were other grays in the herd, none were quite so light in color as she was, and above her lip she had a tuft of thicker hair that looked like a mustache. Before my mother and I had left for this trip, I promised myself that I would not get attached to any individual horse. I had done enough research over the past few years to know and understand their likely futures. But the response that seems to be in the genes of all animal-loving humans, no matter how professional, took over before I had the chance to rein it in. Back on our first day at this field, my mother and I had stayed long after dark, and I sat and talked to Eden, scratching her shoulders and running my hands over the veins on her stomach. I pressed my ear there, listening and talking to the baby I knew was inside. I found myself wondering about the foal; color, sex, health, and future. "I know one thing," I said. "You have a wonderful mother."

On our last morning, as we rushed to the field, I hoped hard that I would get to see Eden's foal. We pulled over in the grass on the side of the road, distracted only a moment by the call of a sharptail, and then crossed the stream of rainwater and climbed the fence. There Eden was, lying on her side and breathing heavily. My mother ran back to the car to get her camera while I stayed with Eden, but far enough away not to impose. I did not want to interfere with the natural birthing process, and I knew she would be more protective when she had a newborn. So I sat on a distant rock and quietly waited. There was blood on her tail, and her nostrils were open wide, but by the time my mother returned Eden had stood up and walked away. We

stayed a bit longer, hoping she would go back into labor, but it had been a false alarm and our plane was scheduled to leave in two hours.

We waited as long as we could before we had to get back in the car and head to the airport. As we left we noticed a new chestnut foal, probably born only about an hour before we had arrived.

Some older mares have been pregnant many times.

65

Some foals find their legs in odd places.

He bent his knees and crawled under his mother, as if to say, "Let me back in; this world is too cold." Behind him, her placenta hung to the ground, billowing in the wind like a skirt, and I wondered about the difference between birth and death in the world of these horses. I decided that the chestnut foal was right.

Listening to Number 89

RHIANNON PERRY ALWINE

I can't remember a time when I didn't love horses. As a child, I communed with an imaginary herd, pretending I was one of them, but it wasn't until I was thirty years old that I had the opportunity to share life with a real horse. His name was Zoya, and he was the reason that I returned to a gift that I thought I had given up when I said good-bye to childhood.

When I moved to New York in 2001, I had to leave Zoya behind in California, and after a few years he began coming to me in dreams. After one particularly disturbing dream in which I found him with no food or water, I decided it was time to travel to California and visit him. I was devastated to find that the dream had been the truth and that he had indeed been reaching out to me for help. Zoya's communication woke me to the fact of how very real the connection between beings of different species can be and that neither distance nor time need inhibit that connection, something of which I had no doubt when I was a child. It was then that I decided to become attuned to Reiki for the purpose of helping animals. This attunement has opened an ability to listen to the animals once again, and I offer the Reiki energy for their healing.

Those "imaginary" horses with which I spent my childhood have come back, and now I know they were not so imaginary after all. I moved back to California and now have two very special horses in my life. I am on a

A medicine hat foal has a noble heritage.

lifelong journey of learning in which I am "rescued" by horses just by spending time in their presence each day, and I am blessed with the lessons they have to teach. Hopefully, I am becoming a better horse.

Two foals share their journey.

In 2004, I became a volunteer with EARS soon after becoming aware of the plight of the PMU mares and foals and after channeling "Rhiannon Between the Worlds," a story of how horses help us heal. The story compelled me to become involved in rescue and to grow to know horses

Rescued from the feed lot, this slaughter-bound mare awaits her new home.

through their own eyes. I enjoy helping animals and their people through Reiki and long-distance animal communication, and dream of someday founding a sanctuary for healing where horses and people can come together to play, dance, and heal.

PMU foal number 89 reached out to me when I saw his photo on www.foalrescue.com. The following is a conversation I had with him during a series of Reiki and long-distance animal communication sessions we shared together after he arrived at Ray of Light Farm in East Haddam, Connecticut.

Can you see the number shaved into my left side? By springtime when my winter coat has shed, it will no longer be visible; even so, it will have left its mark. I was branded at birth with a number, not a name, because that was what my life was worth. I was only a number, just like my mother. Another kind of number marked our worth, too. A dollar number. The dollars for which my mother's estrogen sold. The dollars' worth of the pounds of flesh on my bones. But instead, by a turn of fortune, my fate was to be different. Instead of the feedlot, I was brought here. I try not to remember now what it felt like to leave my mother at such a young age . . . after such a short time

I was only a number just like my mother . . . I felt safe at her side.

71

Sleep comes at last.

with her. She taught me much in those few short months, but I know there is much more she could have taught me about being Horse. I was with many other foals from the 2007 season when I was separated from my mother. We were each just as confused as the other, and our mothers' cries still rang in our ears long after we had accepted that it was we who were alone together now.

I asked, "Would you like to talk with me and share your story?"

I know you are there listening. I will talk with you. Even though I've grown to accept that I will never see my mother again, and even though the warmth of the bodies of

the other foals who share this space with me is a comfort, we are all scared and I am lonely. If I had been with my mother longer, I would know more of what it is to be Horse, and I would know if this feeling of fear is just a natural part of being Horse, or if it is mine alone. Are you ever scared?

The mare hesitates and gives a final look before leaving the trailer.

73

Foals comfort each other.

"Yes, I am. We are all scared at times. It's not just a feeling that you alone experience."

I want for the feeling of safety. Somehow, I know that there is safety when a horse is more than one alone. I felt safe when I was with my mother. I never wanted to move very far from her side. We were in a field with many other mothers and their foals. It was green and fresh and beautiful and as I grew, I learned

to play with those other foals. We played bravely, but not very far away from the safety of our mothers' sides.

Relaxing after a
long trip to safety.

It all changed suddenly with no preparation, no explanation, only confusion and uncertainty about what was to become of us. I remember the long ride that brought us here, and I can still feel the endless motion and our search for balance as we rode and shifted our stances together while the miles passed beneath our hooves. Over the long hours, we began to move in a more uniform balance; cooperating in a common unity, riding the vibrations that came loud and intrusively through the walls and floor of the trailer, numbing our fear with the passing of the long hours.

The number shaved into the side of this foal is the farmer's method of identification.

I welcome that you have made contact. Right now, I don't feel so alone.

I wanted a name for this horse. I could not bear to think of him only by the number on his side. "I want to give you a name. Would you help me?"

A name may help me know myself.

"You have a big heart. A very big heart."

I don't feel very big. I feel small. I feel that I want to be in your pocket.

"Do you know your name already?"

I just heard "Braveheart."

76

As he spoke to me and I looked at his picture, I heard the word "Braveheart," too. I said, "You have a big, brave heart. And you are beautiful."

It is good to know you are there.

I asked him about where he was at that moment.

It is cold. It is early night. My breath comes out in warm steam and I can hear the sound of the others eating nearby. We like this time of day.

The old feelings are farther away, as if the doors have partially closed to their memory. But they have only partially closed. I am still on the edge of fear, and so I stay in the present, with the sound of each mouthful of food, each breath against

This awesome mare has had many foals.

the cold night air, and know the closeness of the others who share this place. We live for quiet.

This puzzled me. I asked, "What do you mean, you live for quiet?"

Quiet is a smooth, soft feeling of assurance. The night is quiet. The dark sky is quiet. And quiet is also the light of day and a warm sun on your back. We like our people quiet, too. Quiet is not fear. There are only two ways of knowing. Quiet and fear.

My mother told me that there are some humans who can be trusted. This is a story that has been passed on and kept alive through generations of horses. My mother had not experienced this trust herself, but she made sure that the story was passed on to each of her foals. She believed that someday one of us would know this trust firsthand. I hope I am the one.

Tears came to my heart as I heard him talk about the horse's great strength to believe in the worthiness of humans. "You have an important gift to give, Braveheart. You are young, but I feel that you have an important mission to fulfill and that you will fulfill it. When you have experienced the worst that can possibly happen, you must take that pain and turn it into the best that can happen. You can do that, Braveheart. For your mother and all like her. For all the foals who didn't have your turn of fate. You will go on to trust and love and to bring Horse to human. As you grow, you will know your mission of healing with those who cross your path. You are already doing that."

I still talk with Braveheart. He tells me there is a human he is watching. Someone he is, perhaps, beginning to trust. Like all those other foals that have been blessed with the miracle of a happy ending, Braveheart is beginning to live with new possibilities and has become part of the healing that happens when we reach out with love and experience the wonder of how "rescues rescue us."

Proud.

A warm embrace.

Number 24—A Leap of Faith

Tiffany DeMartin

We weren't looking to change our lifestyle drastically. We didn't know we were unhappy with the comfortable suburban life that we'd fallen into. We never noticed the dull ache to connect to the natural world until our routine stopped and life as we knew it was replaced with the delicious sensation of burying our hands in the filthy winter coats of three small PMU foals. The baby steps we'd thought we were taking as we moved a handful of rescued chickens and these three foals into the barn of our new home (a farm at the other end of town! The extended family was befuddled!) turned out to be the single greatest blind leap of faith we'd ever taken as a family. And one that we have never regretted.

I have a photo of my husband and myself taken seconds after we hung up with Frank Weller, founder of EARS, and I realized that we would be horse owners in a matter of days. Frank had directed us to his website. We scrolled through photos of the newest batch of foals. "Just looking," we had said. And we were. We had visited countless farm sanctuaries (we were determined that every animal on our farm would be a rescue) and met so many farm animals with so many harrowing stories that it was becoming hard to narrow our search at all. But one thing was absolutely certain. "No horses!" I had said from the beginning.

Tiffany, Rob, and Augusta with Plenti Coup.

I had ridden competitively as a young adult. I had shipped my horses up and down the east coast and handed them off to grooms at the end of the day. I had started as a kid in Pony Club riding bareback through the back hills of my hometown. In those days, I didn't even own tack, and the horse we leased was an old BLM mustang that I rode with a halter and lead line. It was paradise. But somewhere along the way it all got away from me. I found myself competing. It was all about people, ribbons, appearances, and had very little to do with horses. My simple love of horses had gotten tangled up with a dislike for everything surrounding them. All I really wanted was to lie with my back

along the spine of some big reliable friend and watch the clouds roll by. More than twenty years had passed, and the memories still left a bitter taste in my mouth. I wasn't going there again.

But there he was.

In the quickly snapped photo on the website, number 24 was standing in a dreary holding pen with his front legs up on a slab of concrete. His front end was slightly higher than the back and his head turned toward the camera. Never mind that the number "24" was crudely shaved into his thick grey coat, and that the landscape around him suggested things may not be very comfortable. Number 24 looked like a kid

> He's scared, he's alone. The train's already pulled out . . .

Plenti Coup, Arrow, and Doughnut.

sitting on his bags at the train station after a hard trip. He's scared, he's alone. The train's already pulled out, but he's got on his best clothes and he's waiting there for family that he knows will come and get him. Maybe they just got stuck in traffic.

I fell in love. The photo that we snapped of ourselves is a record of the very beginning of the craziest and most profound thing we've ever done for our family. We knew nothing about raising foals. Really nothing about being responsible for horses at all. Grooms had done all my dirty work, and my husband's experience with animals stopped at the occasional family cat.

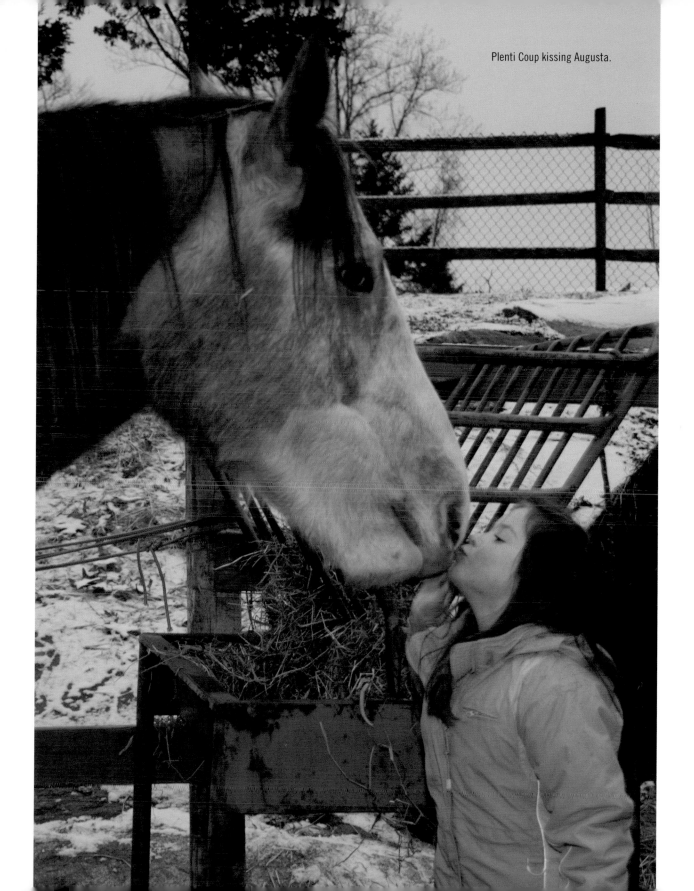

Plenti Coup kissing Augusta.

Augusta and Arrow.

It was late November. At Frank's request, we drove three hours north to a small paddock in the middle of a field and stood for hours in the cold with number 24 and forty other foals. They were all of them wild. They ran from us with fear in their eyes. It took hours to try to gently load our foal, and when we finally did, in a messy clattering of scrambling hooves, he whinnied the most sorrowful cry. We begged Frank to load another just to keep him company and he loaned us a foal that he had earmarked to be kept and trained by EARS: a lovely Belgian filly that was bottle fed and beautifully mannered and helped to ease our colt's fears on the long drive home.

The rest of the story is so personal and so significant to us that it's almost impossible to contain in a short essay. Who knew shoveling manure on a hot summer day could be so cathartic? Or how good that warm soft

The delicious sensation of burying our hands in the filthy winter coats of PMU foals.

nose would feel, after weeks of coaxing, as it tentatively blows on the side of your face for the first time? My daughters, who are four and one year old, and I spent the coming winter walking to the barn in the dark each night after dinner. Our evening routine included feeding the horses, checking the chickens, and then listening for night creatures we had never known were just outside our window. Owls, coyotes, and all sorts of living things welcomed us to their nightly routines. A whole new world opened up to us.

Eventually, we ended up with three foals. Frank had asked us to foster a little paint colt that was quiet when he first arrived. He hung his head and faced the fence for weeks. Who were we kidding? We adopted him almost instantly. Number 24, who has since earned the name Plenti Coup, grew into the most kind and handsome blue roan Clydesdale yearling ever. And, well, we stole Frank's beautiful Belgian right out from under him! We fell in love with her and promised Frank we'd give him ample visitation rights. He finally succumbed and we adopted her, too.

And so began the sometimes painful, sometimes funny, and always humbling learning curve of owning horses. Here we are at dawn on a summer Sunday morning, all of us running in our pajamas down the fairways of the local golf course after our

Tiffany plays with Plenti Coup—a leap of faith.

Opposite: Augusta and Tiffany get a lift from Plenti Coup.

Tiffany and Plenti Coup fall in love.

foals have found a way out of the field. Here we are extracting our foals from the chicken coop after all three had gotten stuck in the doorway while trying to get at a few small handfuls of chicken scratch. Here we are in tears stroking the sweaty neck of a colicky horse who kept us up all night, praying and watching for his recovery. In the crash course of life, we learned how to hitch a trailer, clean and dress wounds, mix mashes of applesauce and bran, tie a makeshift halter from a scrap of rope, and unload a flatbed of more than two hundred bales of hay in fifteen minutes flat. We went to important meetings, to the market, and to school with leftover bits of carrots in our pockets and straw in our hair. We always smelled a little of the barn. We were never happier.

Having horses means so many different things to so many people. Our horses aren't pedigreed. You will never read about them or see them in any publication of record. But the achievements our horses have made have enriched our lives in a way that makes them true champions. We've fostered nearly thirty horses now. And we've watched animals strike out, bite, kick, and carry on. Give these animals time and patient training, and they will always overcome their fears and develop into confident, wonderful companions. When you gain trust, it's a gift they give to you. It's a gift that comes from pulling yourself out of your skin and listening to what they have to say—connecting to the natural world, not dominating it.

We've coaxed seeds to sprout from the bare earth and watched them bud and bloom and bear fruit just outside our kitchen window. We've reared spring chicks in the basement and baked cakes and cookies and breads from the eggs they gave us the following summer. And we've watched countless foals scatter from the trailer and run from us in fear down to the lower field. And with each one that eventually turns and heads in our direction, takes the first cube of sugar from our palm, or wiggles a lip when his belly is first scratched, we've had a glimpse into the great order of the universe that includes all living things. We're always amazed that our seeds grow into plants and that our chickens actually do come home to roost each evening. And we're humbled every time that a foal overcomes his fears and allows a halter to slip over his head, or tempers her reaction when our toddler leans over the fence with a fistful of dandelions.

We never knew this was our idea of perfection. But we think that number 24 did. And we're so glad he found us.

And with each one that eventually turns his head in our direction . . . we've had a glimpse into the great order of the universe that includes all living things.

Beautiful Boys—Jasper and Rudi

CAROLYN DeFASIO

The first time I met Frank Weller, he gave me a hug and a green bracelet with the phrase "Rescues Rescue Us" printed on it. He spoke passionately about the rescue of PMU foals, and left me thinking for weeks about all EARS did to help these forgotten horses.

Months later, when I agreed to foster two yearlings, I noticed that he often ended his e-mails with the phrase "Rescues rescue us," or another one of his favorites, "For the foals." Again he left me thinking.

When the yearlings, Jasper and Rudi, arrived, I was so excited. There were lots of questions from my horse friends, the most common one being, "Is he paying you to do this?" It didn't surprise me that I got some very strange looks when I answered, "No!" But I was shocked and hurt when I e-mailed my best friend from high school to tell her about what I was doing, and she replied with one word: "Sucker!" I had been sure that she, of all people, would understand. After all, when we were growing up together, she had walked beside me on weekends, an hour each way, so that we could watch other people ride until we had enough money saved to ride ourselves. We rode trails together every chance we had, even skipping school sometimes. How could she not understand my commitment when she was the most horse-obsessed person I knew?

Rudi surveys his
new home.

I learned to ignore them all, and I enjoyed fostering the boys. It made me happy just to watch these yearlings graze and it made me laugh when they played, but surprisingly it was while cleaning Rudi's stall that I smiled and said aloud to myself, "This is the best thing I've ever done!"

How was this different from the obsession I already had for my own two horses? My horses are my own selfish pleasure, but these boys . . . I try to explain it by saying that you have to choose the type of person you want to be, especially when it costs you your preciously rare free time—and

some extra bags of grain—every week. I had to ask myself, do I want to be someone who just complains when I see an injustice? Or do I want to be someone who evaluates my resources and then does something about it? I'm proud to be part of a network of people who see these beautiful animals as worth saving and works hard to rescue them. But the best part came when Katie, one of those people who gave me strange looks last year, came up to me at work to tell me that I had inspired her to take in an abused dog to rehabilitate. She smiled at me with a gleam in her eyes and said she, too, now understood why.

When the yearlings and Rudi arrived, I was so excited.

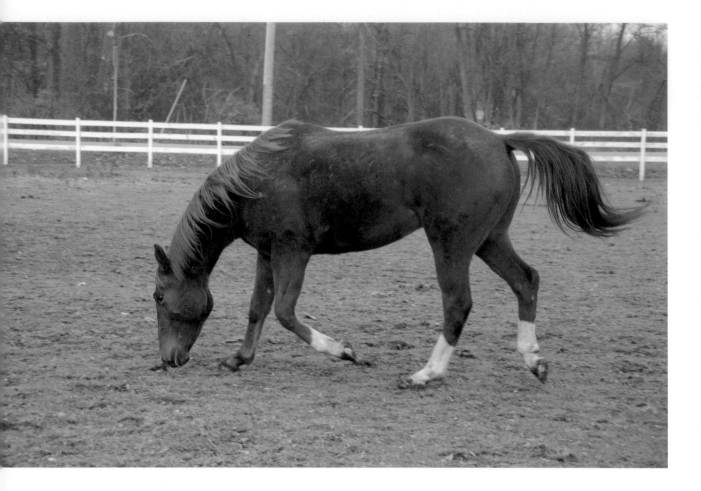

"This is the best thing I have ever done," says Carolyn.

When I read in the papers about the twelve horses confiscated by the SPCA after they were nearly starved, or about the person who tied his dog to a tree before setting it on fire, I realize that while I was not able to help those souls, I do know of two beautiful horses that didn't end their lives in a slaughterhouse, in part because I was brave enough to risk being a "sucker." I've seen that I can make a difference, not only in the lives of these foals, but also in the lives of friends like Katie and the dog that she took in. The knowledge that I've made even a small difference gives me a more optimistic view of life. When I

think of the potential of many people each making a small difference, then I feel even more positive about the future. Sure, there are terrible things in the news, but there are also people, like Frank Weller and Katie the dog rescuer, who make an important choice to save animals. For me, being a part of this makes it easier to get up in the morning and enjoy the day to the fullest. That's when I understand how rescues rescue us, and I wish that I could do more.

Beautiful boy—
Rudi.

97

Foals like to dance and prance and try out their new legs.

Love

Buckskin filly watches for Mom.

Angels Among Us

FRANK WELLER

In each of the more than two hundred and fifty adoptions that EARS has completed, it is easy to see how excited and uplifted the new family becomes. In some cases, the family has an autistic child or a family member challenged with disability. In those cases, the relationship is so obviously therapeutic. The connection with a foal or mare lifts the whole family beyond its perceived limits. There are definite medical benefits. Some children who were previously withdrawn feel safe when having a relationship with an equine. They start to connect

This two-day-old foal relaxes near Mom.

Mom gives a kiss to
her new foal.

to other parts of their world. Many types of therapy use horses for the treatment of adults and children.

In many cases, a teen or preteen child finds the horse to be the only living soul that will listen to his or her problems, and he or she feels safe conversing with the horse. It is a relationship of trust and love that is beyond words. That scenario works really well for adults, too. The unspoken connection with a horse bonds all the families we have known to become stronger and happier together. We see these rescued equines as angels among us.

Overcoming Fear—Thomas and Rasa

Jennifer Milavsky

Each started life without a name, known only by a number. Now they are known as Thomas and Rasa, the ponies, our babies. They have names.

It was an eventful two months. My husband, Glen, and I (mostly my husband) had worked from dawn through dusk to clear land and build a barn to bring home my mare. I had boarded her for years and years, and now it was finally time for her to come home. She had been my passion even before my husband. I could not wait to have her in my own backyard. Glen had worked tirelessly to make her a home. He cleared land, milled lumber, and erected a barn, all in six weeks' time. There were just a couple of obstacles. First, my mare needed a companion. Second, my husband had always been afraid of horses.

We met the foals on a warm spring day. We had looked at hundreds of foals online over the course of several months, and had already visited more than twenty other foals over the past few weekends. It had been a long drive. There were three foals in a large paddock eating hay. Their foster caretaker had named them Thomas, Hope, and Bromley. We had made the drive to meet a specific foal, Bromley. As we approached the fence line, two of the foals came straight over to greet us, but not the one we had been there to meet. From that moment on, we knew that we belonged together. We spent hours with them that day and had to tear ourselves away to make the difficult drive home.

My husband, Glen, had always been afraid of horses.

I will never forget the instant my husband met Thomas. It was love at first sight. They seemed to belong together. Glen scratched and petted him, kissed his nose, and gave him soft raspberries. Thomas could not get enough of it. They played tag, and Thomas followed him around like a puppy. They looked like little kids having the time of their lives. I would swear to you that Thomas and Glen share the same sense of humor. If horses could smile, I would have seen a beaming smile on Thomas's face that day as they played. I found myself bonding strongly to Thomas as well, but I also felt drawn to the filly.

She was very different from Thomas. She was very gentle and serious. She spent the whole afternoon with her face gently pressed against me. She followed me everywhere without ever being pushy. I had the feeling that she had the potential to be spectacular. She wanted to be loved so much, and she wanted to give everything she had in return for that love.

Those two foals also seemed to belong together. They were never more than a few inches away from each other, while the third foal in the paddock wanted nothing to do with them. If Thomas went to investigate, Hope was not far behind. If one foal rolled, they both rolled. They nuzzled each other and groomed each other. They lined up shoulder to shoulder to walk across the paddock. In the end, we did not have the heart to separate them. Although we had only built a two-stall barn, we agreed to adopt both.

Thomas and Hope came home two weeks later. They arrived in the middle of the night, in the pouring rain, with thunder booming overhead. Despite the terrible storm, Frank Weller from EARS had found his way to our little country home with his two-horse stock trailer, bearing license plates that boldly stated "FOALS." They made their way down the long driveway, through the gardens in the backyard, through the paddock, and into their new stall. They were not quite halter-broke and there were no electric lights to guide the way, just an occasional flash of far-off lightning and the soft reassurance of our voices coaxing them to follow us. Once safely in their stall, and after much hugging, kissing, and cooing, we fluffed up their bedding and made sure their water was topped off. They had a few bites of hay, curled up together, and went to sleep.

> From that moment on, we knew we belonged together.

In the morning Hope was renamed Rasa, short for "tabula rasa," or "clean slate" in Latin, as we felt it fit her better. As time has passed we have realized how well it does match her personality. She came to us with no bad habits—really, no habits or training at all. She was totally open to

Our babies seem to grow a little bit every day.

everything. She seems to want to learn everything we strive to teach her, and she learns so quickly, soaking in everything like a sponge. Rasa is so eager to please and always looks like she is taking notes on what we have asked her to do, writing it down on her tablet so she can study it later. Although alternate names were suggested, none fit Thomas better than that. His foster family originally named him after a well-known children's cartoon train. Watching him move around his new paddock, the train analogy seemed to suit him. He is short and stout. He throws his front legs out ahead of him like he is a gaited carriage horse. It brings to mind images of steam trains from old movies, chugging along, very rhythmic and very strong.

A week later my mare, Nexxie, came home. She had always been high strung and nervous. She was brutally jealous of anyone or anything I went near, person, animal, or object. Nexxie had a strong obsession with me. She did not play well with others. She had been known, on more than one occasion, to tear down the walls of her stall to get to me. Fire always burned in her eyes. Nexxie was never at ease. The day I walked her off the trailer, she walked quietly into the paddock. She investigated her new stall and then she looked over at Thomas and Rasa. I was surprised to see her gaze turn soft and gentle. Nexxie immediately knew the babies were hers and that she was finally home. It was as if she had been waiting her whole life for that very moment, and her life would never be the same. She has been at ease since first setting eyes on them. She has never been jealous of Thomas or Rasa. In fact, she shares our time freely with them.

It is now three years later. Our babies seem to grow a little bit every day. Life has changed drastically for me and my husband. We seem to have a never-ending number of daily chores to do. Our time is no longer our own; we share it with all our babies. We would not trade it for the world.

Thomas and Rasa are the most wonderful horses I have ever met. Thomas has personality to spare and the best sense of humor I have ever

encountered. He will follow us anywhere and would like to be included in everything that we do. He loves to cuddle and be scratched. When he is super comfortable, as you stand to admire him, he loves to open his lips, rest his teeth gently on your forehead, and drool down your face. Rasa is gentle and thoughtful and eager to please. She will follow us with her nose at our shoulders for hours. I believe both of them think they are just plain old lap dogs. They love to be close to us, to be scratched and groomed. They love just being with us. My husband may still be afraid of horses in general, but he never shows it when working with ours. He and Thomas are great friends. He can jump up on Thomas, sit on him, lie on him, even stand

Our time is no longer our own. We share it with all of our babies. And we wouldn't trade it for the world!

The mare is always alert.

on him. Thomas is always happy to oblige, and that friendship builds confidence.

When Glen and I first made the decision to adopt these foals, we understood we were saving their lives. With three years' perspective I can say that when we brought these two foals home and into our lives, we did more than that. We rescued my beloved mare as well. I had always given her everything I thought she needed. She had food, water, shelter; she had blankets and toys. She had great care and all-day pasture turnout. Most of all, she had my love and affection. That made her body comfortable, but not her mind. Nexxie did not rest comfortably and she was not complete until she came back home to the love of Thomas and Rasa, our expanded family.

Joy of Life—Joy and Jacinto

LESLIE ANN MIGENES

Who would have ever thought that while sitting on a train at seven o'clock in the morning my father would come across an advertisement for foals in need of a good home? We never imagined that this ad would change our family's lives forever. But this is exactly how we learned about these special foals and their need for a good home. My father, Harry Migenes, found an advertisement about foals needing adoption while he was waiting on the platform for his commuter train. He read that a shipment of PMU foals had come in from Canada to a rescue sanctuary in Connecticut, where we live. He had no idea what a PMU foal was but decided to call me anyway, because he knew that I was always dreaming about horses. My college classes hadn't started for the day, but I jumped out of bed so that I could go to the website to see if the information was legitimate. Excitement flooded my body. *Could this be it, the moment our dream comes true?* Like an eager child, I skipped all the words on the website and went straight for the pictures. I scrolled down. There were about a dozen horses before I saw her, standing tall and proud, the new love of my life, foal 05-27. She was a paint filly with black and white spots, and I just had to have her.

As the youngest member of my family, I have shared a love for horses with my dad since I was three years old. I have ridden on and off since I was seven, and I have always enjoyed being in the presence of horses. The

As soon as I saw her my heart filled with joy, and so the name stayed because I knew that Joy would be the joy of my life.

prospect of rescuing a horse and having one in my life seemed like it would be the fulfillment of my dreams. I hoped to start a sanctuary to rescue and rehabilitate unwanted and abused animals.

I called my dad back and he advised me to call the sanctuary to investigate the program more fully. But he said I shouldn't get too attached to the horse I saw on the Internet. "Don't start thinking of names for her," he warned. I left a message with Frank Weller at the sanctuary, hoping to find out if she was still available. I couldn't let little Viva (I had already named her) get away.

Yes, foal 05-27 was still available. I knew in my heart that she was the one for me and that my dream of owning a horse was going to become a reality. My mother Lydia and I would go to EARS right away to check out the foals. If this trip was successful, we would then bring my dad on the weekend.

My mom and I drove an hour from Easton to New Milford on that January day. When we arrived, Frank brought us out to meet foal 05-27. I asked him what they called her, and he replied, "Joy." I decided right then and there that I hated the name Joy and that her new name was going to be Viva, which means "live" in Spanish. Frank led us to a circular paddock and there she was, standing pitifully on the opposite end of the ring. She was shy, and unlike the other horse sharing the paddock with her, she was not friendly. But I knew she was mine. As soon as I saw her, my heart filled with joy, and so the name stayed, because I knew that Joy was going to be the joy of my life. Frank later told me that when he had first got the foals, he asked an animal communicator what impression she received from the horse as to what her name was. The animal communicator responded that it was Joie de Vivre, which in French, of course, means "joy of life."

My mother and I made our journey back home discussing all the possibilities. Even she was excited. She was not too fond of horses. To her, they were too big and they made her nervous. But these little foals were so small even she felt comfortable. This was another hint that this dream was going to come true, because my father had said that we couldn't get a horse unless my mom felt comfortable with the situation. We arrived back at our house, explained everything to my dad, and decided to make another trip so he could see the horse for himself.

The weekend couldn't come soon enough. All three of us were excited, and my sister Olivia, who lives in New York City, even joined us on the trip. As a family we arrived at EARS, looking at all the different horses. Each of us bonded with a different one. I had already bonded to Joy and made the decision that she was to be mine, and my dad found Bailey, a bay colt that had an amazing spirit. Once we found Joy and Bailey, we decided that they were to be ours that day. Together we all sat down with Frank, who had qualified us, and signed the adoption papers. We were now the

113

Opposite: We are now the proud owners of two foals, and we can't be prouder. The horses have been inseparable.

proud owners of two foals, and we couldn't have been happier.

Joy continued to stay in her shell. Her antisocial behavior worried us at times. We wondered if she would ever trust us to go near her. Joy remained cautious, but she was happy and she was safe. Not only did she have her new family, but she had fallen hopelessly in love with Bailey, and he had fallen in love with her as well. The two horses have been inseparable ever since. We would watch the horses hug and kiss as they rolled and played, their happiness adding to our happiness, making everyone content.

I realized that the way to Joy's heart was persistence. I made sure to be outside with her every day, and even though she wouldn't allow me to touch her, she knew that I loved her. Secretly, while she wasn't looking, I would take a brush and then gently whisk it over her coat. Eventually, she learned that I wasn't there to hurt her, and gradually she allowed me to brush certain parts of her body until she gained enough trust to let me brush her all over. Once I had earned Joy's trust, she would wait for me to come outside and visit her. She looked forward to our grooming rituals.

We changed Bailey's name to Jacinto, which is the name of a Spanish saint, after my father had a vivid dream of the horse telling him that was his rightful name. Jacinto proved to be the opposite of our timid and reserved Joy, because he basked in all the attention that we poured out. While Joy hid behind him, he allowed us to brush him and would nuzzle us affectionately every time we gave him a good scratch on the chest.

Joy and Jacinto are currently in training. Joy made a huge turnaround and is a loving and trusting horse that loves to be hugged and kissed. Jacinto is as happy as ever and loves to do anything as long as he can do it with Joy. We feel as if the horses have been part of our family forever. Everyone in the family has benefited from the horses' presence. My mom, who was fearful at first, has grown close to the animals and sings to them often.

We would watch the horses hug and kiss as they rolled and played, and their happiness added to our happiness, making everyone content.

My father spends all of his spare time outside working hard, doing farm duties, and loving every moment of it. And I have an impenetrable bond with both Joy and Jacinto and enjoy the trust that I have earned by working patiently with them. Even our little Pomeranian dogs, Sofie and Gigi, have grown to love the horses and enjoy running up and down the side of the ring barking and wagging their tails.

The horses are at the center of our family's life. My mom, dad, the dogs, and even my sister on trips from the city, all take time out of our busy lives to make time for the horses, and that means we also spend more time with each other. It's been two years since we signed those adoption papers, and our lives are all the richer. The backyard has changed with the addition of a barn, pasture, and a round pen, and our routine has also changed to include feeding, grooming, and training. The horses have created an even stronger bond in our family because despite our different schedules and commitments, we share our love for our horses entirely together. It's amazing that, because of that little ad at the train station, many dreams have come true for us.

Plan A—Capricious and Coco Chanel

LESLIE BALLOTTI

It was a fall evening and I felt like a little girl waiting for Santa on Christmas Eve. I was so excited awaiting the arrival of number 6 and number 34. Finally the trailer with Coco Chanel and Capricious arrived! The two yearlings, weaned from their mothers just days ago, looked so desperate. They didn't know what or who we were and didn't want to leave the stock trailer they were transported in. My four daughters and I were filled with many emotions. The horses were the sweetest, most vulnerable and innocent animals we had ever seen. I was well aware that yearlings could be unpredictable and that no matter what, you should never trust a horse completely, but I felt very confident about these two. My daughters and I offered reassurance, stroking them and talking to them to let them know it was going to be all right.

Other people told me I should send them to Vermont to be trained, but I could not imagine letting them out of my sight. I wanted to be there like I am for my girls, to share in their milestones, knowing when they have a bad day, and seeing what happens when they are happy. A friend in England once told me the English breed their own horses because they want to know what has happened to their horse from day one. It's true; if something scared that horse early on, you'd know it and you could work through it a lot more easily. I entered that dark, open trailer and told them

Capricious has no inhibitions. She doesn't shy at anything. She is a girl in charge.

Leslie with Capricious: "Capricious is a very smart horse and well in tune with her environment."

I would protect them and that they were safe. Capricious came right off and began to wander around. Next was Coco. She was, and still is, more apprehensive. She needs to snort, paw, and nudge things ten times more than Capricious. Only after she saw Capricious nibbling my hair and feeling obviously comfortable around me did she venture out of the trailer.

After a fifteen-minute walk in their halters with my daughters Kiki and Kara carrying the lead ropes, we introduced them to their new horse family. They had five other equine sisters and brothers in their new herd. Everyone accepted each other—well, almost! Through the gate's slots they smelled one another, and our plan for the next day was to use water and vinegar to sponge clean everyone's nostrils. I learned this trick from my milkman in Italy; it's a way to prevent horses from distinguishing strangers. They end up accepting the new horses more quickly.

I'm jumping ahead of myself. First let me tell you the story of how we got Coco into her stall the first night. Used to being out in the herd with very little or no enclosures, Coco refused to enter into her stall. Capricious, no problems. Coco, no way! This was the challenge for the night. "Think, think, think!" I told myself. "Okay, if she can't see the stall then she can't be scared of it. Let's try to blindfold her." No, she didn't want anything to do with blindfolds. Then my daughter Kiki reminded me of what I used to do while riding her horse. The horse was terrified of water, and every time she had to cross a stream, I would get off and back her through it. Using the same philosophy—that if she couldn't see it she wouldn't be scared of it—we did exactly that: we backed Coco into her stall. Perfect, for ten seconds. Then we closed the door and watched Coco jump out of her stall, over my daughter Kiki. Wow, that was amazing! I had never seen a horse jump, from a standstill, over a four-foot wall, let alone over my daughter!

Geoff with Capricious.

From that moment on I did not take anything for granted. When I handled the yearlings, I always would have a plan A, B, C, and even sometimes a plan D ready for action. In this case, plan C was to leave the stall door open and stay in the stall with Coco. We took turns standing in the stall with her and, after about two hours, Coco felt comfortable enough to be alone. That worked so well that the next morning, Coco did not want to leave her stall, and we had to coax her out.

The Ballotti girls.

Opposite: I think Coco is more mature in ways. She could be the liaison in the herd, and everyone loves her.

The next day we also introduced the yearlings to the new herd. I was shocked by how well everyone got along. I was pleased because I like to turn all the horses out together. The only problem I encountered was with my Haflinger mare, Bimba, who was weaning her own filly. Capricious still wanted to take milk so she tried to suckle from the mare, but the mare wouldn't have anything to do with her. In fact, she made it her business to chase Capricious every minute she could. So I separated the yearlings from the rest of the herd, temporarily.

Weeks later, after days of the horses calmly hanging over the fence socializing, I tried it again. They all seemed to be minding their own business, so I decided to clean the water trough. Just seconds later, Capricious found me and charged me to seek

Capricious has a very humanlike personality . . .

protection from Bimba, who was once again chasing her. She knocked me off my feet and I cracked my pelvis in five spots. Ouch, that was painful! From that point on, I was insistent in reminding Capricious that I *would* protect her, but I only have two legs, not four, and I don't weigh eight hundred pounds. Today, she won't leave my side when I come into the barn. She's like a trusty golden retriever and would probably sleep next to me at night if there was space.

People say good things happen to good people, and I feel this is the best thing that has happened to me, second to the birth of my children. Unfortunately, I had found out about EARS because I lost a horse I loved. I had been living in Rome, and when it was time to move back to the United States, I had to organize the transport of a household, children, dogs, and horses. I was planning on bringing back three horses. I came back to the United States first with the children and the household; then I went back to get the dogs and send the horses to Amsterdam for their flight to New York. However, when I arrived back at our Italian home, I learned that the night before, someone had stolen one of my horses! It was Quantana, a Belgian warmblood, who was my grand prix jumper. I was devastated. I couldn't sleep or eat. I was completely heartbroken. I decided to take back my daughter's mare in the space already booked on the plane, so at least I was able to bring three horses home. But the loss of Quantana was like hitting bottom.

Then wonders began to happen. The mare that I took last minute in Quantana's place delivered a foal, Bambi, that we love to pieces. One day I found myself crying over Quantana while visiting a tack shop, and the saleswoman took me out for coffee and told me about her rewarding experience with EARS. She told me that her family's adoption experience changed their lives. I thought that it was important to focus on saving the baby horses that I saw on the EARS website. That effort got me out of the depression that I felt over the loss of Quantana. Today I foster three more horses for the rescue. I feel grateful to have this opportunity to save horses and work with them daily. They teach me patience, understanding, and how to listen. I get the biggest thrill when I see the lightbulb go on for them when I am training. I am always amazed when they learn and understand what I am trying to teach them.

. . . and I believe she has feelings, too.

In the years when I had Quantana, I devoted hours to working on perfecting movements. The competition world of horses was thrilling, but the kind of training I am doing now is very rewarding and gives me

Now, today, she still doesn't leave my side when I come into the barn. She is like the trusty golden retriever. She would probably sleep next to me at night if there was room. She is my pot of gold at the end of the rainbow.

tremendous pleasure. I am a registered nurse specializing in pediatrics, I am a mom, and I have a great respect for horses and animals. With this work I am able to put all my skills, interests, and passions together. Coco Chanel and Capricious have inspired my hope and dream of opening a riding center that uses the rescued horses to help with therapy for mentally and physically challenged children and adults.

Bonding a Family—Boulder Bluff Zane Oberon

Michelle Desroches-Walker

11-12-06

Mom and I met the sweetest four-month-old

Bay Clydesdale, Zane

We want to adopt him

He was saved from slaughter

At three months old

A Premarin foal.

12-4-06

Our family works hard

I am impressed and proud

Of my mom

My husband

My daughter.

Mom single-handedly cleaned the whole house this weekend

Sean single-handedly built two stalls this weekend

Andrea cleaned her room and helped out everyone

I cleaned out every inch of the barn

We just got Zane, the baby Clydesdale

We will name him Oberon, we are so happy!

Boulder Bluff Zane Oberon silently called to us at the equine event last year. He stood in his stall on big fluffy pink feet . . .

12-12-06

Joy encircles me

And my family

Through illness

And health

Happiness has taken residence

In my life—in our lives

Within our home—within our farm

Happiness has bonded us together

Our joy cannot be broken

Not now . . .

Our dreams are here

Among us . . .

We hold each other up

And we hold each of our dreams

As dear.

This morning as we walked with Zane

Sean and I saw a shooting star

It was a momentary

Visual sign of promise

Last night

We all stood beneath

The glowing

Aurora borealis

Our dreams realized

The horses snorted from the barn

Nickering their sweet good-nights to us, and

To baby Boulder Bluff Zane Oberon.

. . . calmly gazing our way with innocent dark brown eyes blinking behind long black lashes.

Boulder Bluff Zane Oberon, our "little" baby Clydesdale, silently called to us at the Equine Affaire last year. He stood in his stall on big fluffy pink feet calmly gazing our way with innocent dark brown eyes blinking behind long black eyelashes. He was only four months old; his hocks touched each other as he faced us beyond the bars of his door. We asked to go into the stall, and we spent much time standing by this gentle, giant baby as he allowed us to walk around him, hug him, and lean on him. It was then that we knew we wanted to take him home. We hated leaving him behind, but we knew we needed to go through the proper adoption channels.

Sandra, Andrea, Zane Oberon, Michelle, and Sean share a moment.

Training Oberon is very rewarding. He is a quick learner.

As soon as we got home, we immediately started filling out the paperwork and pulling together the funds needed to bring him home to us. My husband started right away to build him a very spacious stall, and my daughter couldn't wait for our new foal to come to us. Oberon arrived in the trailer, all four feet splayed out like a large Bambi, scared yet trusting. He warily stepped out of the truck. Yet as soon as he set his feet on our driveway he was ready to be part of our family. We must have checked on him a hundred times that first night, and he seemed relieved to see us each time. Friends and family visited just to see the baby Clydesdale. The miniature horses befriended him. It is amazing to see Oberon at one thousand pounds grooming the withers of a two- or three-hundred-pound miniature horse. He didn't disappoint anyone with his kind disposition and large size.

Training Oberon is very rewarding, because he is such a quick learner. Still a yearling as I write this, he responds predictably to commands: walk, trot, canter, whoa, stand, back, give, turn, and eat. He is a gentleman and gives each of his hooves when requested. He takes a saddle as easily as a blanket; he takes the bridle as if it were a halter. He runs to us like a child, and when he canters, the ground shakes. He grew four inches in one week! At one and a half years old he is already at least sixteen hands high. He seems to run in slow motion through the snow; his feathers appear to float like the clouds.

He is learning to wear the harness; we attached bells to his harness during the holidays and let him loose in the corral. I whistled "Winter Wonderland" as he trotted with the rhythmical, "Jingle, jingle, jingle, jingle."

He seems to run in slow motion, and his feathers appear to float like clouds. He is truly an awesome sight!

133

Andrea pets Oberon.
He is a gentleman.
He is the pride and
joy of our farm.

We all can't wait until he is old enough to harness up and go for a drive through the snow in a one-horse open sleigh. Oberon is an angel to our family. We couldn't imagine life without him, as he is the pride and joy of our little farm.

He is a true angel and we are so glad to have him as part of our family. We couldn't imagine life without him.

Rene has been riding Tally Ho for more than five years.

Hope

Blossoming

FRANK WELLER

Horses, like people, can bloom where they are planted. They even bring their own fertilizer. The most important ingredients, however, are love and trust, but beyond that is training. We owe it to these horses to take that final step with them. There are many styles of training that work, but the successful ones seem to understand that each horse is an individual. That awareness guides the trainer to find the best key to unlock the horse's potential. Seeing things from a horse's point of view can certainly accelerate the process. The results can be stunning. Training can enhance the relationship between horse and human. With time and patience, training increases the conversation and the connection.

Horses become partners in work and in play. We have seen them blossom into athletes, ambassadors, and solid citizens of the world. We encourage people to enjoy the rewarding pursuit of training for their own enrichment and for the betterment of the equine. A famous trainer told us, "You are always training your horse . . . for better or for worse." With faithful training, PMU horses are blossoming for all to appreciate.

Imagine waking up at 2:30 a.m. on a Sunday morning. The normal world will probably sleep in until 10:00 or 11:00 a.m. Shaking off the chilly morning air, you go out to feed your horse and you may even have to wake him up. After the morning rituals, you go to hook up the trailer, having made preparations

Renee and Tally are ranked fourth in the nation.

Renee and Tally are truly a team, relying on each other to achieve athletic success.

the night before. You load your horse and drive two hours for a 7:30 a.m. start time to be judged in a dressage ring.

Many equine competitors do that and more all over the country. Renee Stefanko has been riding Dakota, also known as Tally Ho, for more than five years. Renee and Tally are riding at the beginning novice level of eventing, and have been ranked as high as fourth in the nation. The three phases—dressage, cross country, and stadium jumping—make for a long day. Tally loves it. He goes happily from one test to the next. Renee and Tally are truly a team, relying on each other to achieve ongoing athletic success. Renee does a great job of feeding, training, transporting, and loving Tally. Tally, however, not only does

140

all that Renee asks of him, but he makes up for her mistakes. If she misses a spot while taking a jump, his athletic ability covers the extra distance or, if short, allows him to pop over a jump. He knows the dressage test as well as she does and has often guided her through a lapse of concentration.

He goes happily from one task to the next.

That is what teamwork is all about, helping each other along the way. This team is more than just horse and rider, or even rescued and rescuer—they are friends that love working together. Their friendship is blossoming as fruitfully as their athletic ability, and Tally Ho is a great example of the heights that PMU horses can achieve.

Healing Grace—Diamond and Puck

DEBORAH BUCKENDORF-COLE

In July of 2003, Frank Weller, a longtime friend, told us about the plight of the PMU foals. Prior to talking with him, my husband Craig and I hadn't a clue about the cruel fate of the pregnant mares that were hooked up to urine collection equipment. To say the least, we were shocked and angered when we also learned of the slaughter of thousands of innocent foals who were born to those pregnant mares. After we came to understand this situation, all we knew was that we needed to help, in whatever way we could.

Craig and I had been fighting our own battle for a few years. We were fatigued by a long journey to find answers for his ill health. Then, there was a surprise diagnosis of a brain tumor. It devastated us. The drugs given to shrink the tumor did not succeed. Surgery followed. A dazzling array of doctors, therapists, and focus drugs proved Craig was very lucky, in the scheme of things; he was alive! However, he was left with traumatic brain injury, also known as TBI. Although his particular deficits are considered to be mild now, Craig will admit that in the spring of 2002 he felt as if "All the king's horses and all the king's men couldn't put Humpty together again." But come October 2003, it only took two tiny PMU foals to glue a challenged man and his frayed wife back together again!

We paid Mr. Weller to rescue two foals from the PMU foal auction that September. Sight unseen, we offered to foster them until he found

Deb and Diamond: There is a profound psychological connection that seems to touch everyone in the presence of an equine.

They are no longer babies; except to us, of course.

proper parents. Clearly this was a crazy leap of faith. Patty Wahlers at H.O.R.S.E. of Connecticut loaned us Boogie, a wise, old retired police horse, to teach our scared babies how to become confident horses. Patty, our trainer Karen White, and Frank all pitched in to support our fostering efforts. However, we wondered how we'd find the strength to give them up when the time came.

Just days after their arrival at our home, I looked outside to see what they were doing, and there was Craig sitting on the ground between them. He had the sweetest smile on his face, and with good reason. Both foals had their mouths on either side of my husband's head: little Puck was licking the left side of Craig's head, and our Diamond was licking the right. In that moment we both knew those two little baby horses weren't going

Both foals had their mouths on either side of my husband's head.

anywhere! Healing seemed to take place within Craig when he was in their presence—a grounding of sorts. They forced us to live only in the moment when we were with them, which was a great cognitive exercise for Craig. It's been good for me, too. It's not just because horses are powerful animals and can be dangerous; it's that those who know horses come to believe in their psychic ability, if you will. They embody a clear intent so pure and honest that they command one's immediate attention.

Once we learned our horses' language, they learned ours. We knew if they were having an off day, sometimes by the way they ate their breakfast and sometimes by the way they walked out of their stalls and into the pasture. They in turn could tell if we were sullen or having a gloomy day, and would come up to either of us in turn and stand near as if to say, "How can I help?" We could communicate beyond words with gesture, touch, and thought. If I thought about meeting Puck and Diamond on the fence line, I would picture it in my mind, and they would be there when I arrived. That intimate communication made for great trail rides and instructive ring work. We shared dark days and joyous days, but because we were bonded together, each day was a blessing.

When I volunteered at an equine rescue in Connecticut, I had the pleasure of witnessing the effects horses have on Alzheimer's patients and seniors in a nursing home. We used to bring horses and ponies to visit because of the revitalizing effects they had on the patients. In one instance, a nurse at the facility told us a particular patient hadn't spoken in weeks. But when a miniature pony named Endora, who is locally famous for her hospital visits, walked up to the frail woman, that woman smiled, spoke sweetly to the pint-sized creature, petted her, and even fed her carrots! The nurses felt that it was a therapeutic milestone for that woman.

Similar effects of heightened awareness can be seen at the We Will Ride Therapeutic Riding Program in North Salem, New York. As a vol-

unteer there, I have seen challenged children respond in many positive ways just by seeing the horses, being near them, or when anticipating sitting on the back of a horse during their therapy sessions. They became more confident in relating to people, more focused on the task at hand, and, in general, their spirits were lifted. As Winston Churchill said, "There is something about the outside of the horse that is good for the inside of a man."

The once-frightened foals have grown into magnificent, contented horses.

Our amazing horses are four years old now. They are no longer babies, except to us, of course. The once frightened, unwanted foals, saved from an auction bound for slaughter, have grown into magnificent, contented horses. They've been trained and happily go for rides. Believe it or not, they know they were rescued—they know they are loved. In turn, they rescued us with their healing grace. Sharon Ralls Lemon said, "The essential joy of being with horses is that it brings us in contact with the rare elements of grace, beauty, spirit, and fire." Simply put, Puck and Diamond returned these rare elements to us when we needed them the most. These elements had been in our lives before Craig's illness, but our fears of him not recovering had depleted our reserves. Fear had somehow overturned grace, and our sense of beauty in all things. It had stolen our joyous spirit—our fire had gone out. We were so busy looking in one direction that we lost sight of the big picture.

Our horses made us see in them what had fallen away from us. Since the day they came into our lives they have given us centering joy. Life is more balanced. Yes, horses need a great deal of care, and they are a lot of work. But if you enjoy what you do, you never work a day in your life! So who rescued who? For us, our time with them is a privilege, graceful therapy, and an immense amount of fun. What a wonderful journey this has been.

Slaughter Bound—Savannah Belle

NANCY GOLDMARK

I used to think that it was trite when people who rescued animals said, "I didn't rescue him; he rescued me." Well, I now apologize to all those people because the same thing happened to me.

I bought Hawk Eye in February 1994 and immediately declared the day I bought him as his birthday, since his real date of birth was unknown. In fact, most everything about him was unknown. No papers, no show name, and no knowledge of his life before he was five years old. He was an eleven- to twelve-year-old jumper, seventeen hands, a Trakhener/ Thoroughbred cross, and the fulfillment of my lifelong desire to own a horse. I had said to my husband in conversation one day that all my childhood fantasies had been met except one—I never had a horse. His response was that if my childhood fantasy was to be tall and blonde, he couldn't help me, but he certainly could get me a horse!

So I went horse shopping, met Hawk Eye at the first barn, rode him once, and said, "He's the one!" And that was the beginning of a fourteen-year relationship that was wonderful from the day it began. I spent a part of almost every day with him in rain, sleet, ice, snow, and heat. We had a bond that was so strong that I knew when he was under the weather without a vet, when he was going to spook before he did, and when just a hack in the woods was all he wanted to do. He was a discerning horse who didn't warm up to everyone, but if he loved you, he loved you like no other.

This past August, my healthy twenty-six-year-old Hawk Eye, who had been retired for about a year due to failing eyesight and just because he deserved it, had a mild-to-severe episode of colic. After staying up all night with him and our barn manager, we shipped him by trailer to his vet at Rhinebeck Equine. He stayed for several days to be tested and examined, and each day I drove up and spent the day with him. The vets couldn't find anything wrong and so he returned home, feeling better but without a diagnosis. Three days later he came in from turnout with severe belly pain, unable to stand up, sweating profusely, and going into shock, so he was shipped to the closest vet. This time, as I followed the trailer, I knew that we were in big trouble. By the time we got to the clinic, he was down in the trailer. And this time the ultrasound showed a shadow of a tumor in his small intestine. I made the decision not to put him through the agony of surgery. As he lay on the grass and was euthanized in my arms, I literally felt his spirit leave his body. He fought it a bit and I whispered in his ear, "Go, Hawk Eye. I will be okay. Just be out of pain."

His cremation and the burial of his ashes followed a few weeks later, but I was bereft. My mind was comfortable with my decision, yet I felt so sad for weeks on end. When I packed away his things, and took off the stall sign from his door, it was hard and I thought I would never have another horse.

But as time went on, I was still drawn to the barn. It made me feel better to be there, not worse. After about two months, I started to entertain the idea of buying a new horse, possibly a Clydesdale. I started to e-mail breeders, thought about attending the World Clydesdale Festival in Wisconsin, and rode one to see if I was comfortable. But the PMU situation kept pulling at my heartstrings. I asked Frank Weller to keep an eye out for

a PMU Clyde. He pointed me to the "Slaughter-Bound" page of his rescue website, which showed foals in immediate jeopardy in the feedlot. I went to the site, took one look at "SB #14" and said, "That's the one!"

There was something about this yearling that just connected with me. She is a Clydesdale (sire) Paint (dam) cross, one and a half years old. The adoption was arranged and finalized, but the waiting seemed interminable! She finally was shipped thirty-six hours to Pennsylvania with eighteen other horses, where she was met by Frank and the Ray of Light Farm gang. (Ray of Light Farm is another hard-working rescue that teamed up with EARS.) From there it was a ten-hour

I have been to see her a few times already, and each time she is a little less wary and more responsive to me.

151

ride to Connecticut, where she remained for a couple of weeks in quarantine before she could come home to my barn.

I went to see her a few times, and each time she was a little less wary and more responsive to me. I named her Savannah Belle (using the SB that once stood for slaughter-bound). She was adorable, sassy, and smart, I could see that already, and I couldn't wait to be a part of her life. It was a leap of faith—she had no pedigree, no papers, I didn't know if she was a "good mover," and didn't even really know her temperament. She had not been vetted or ridden or x-rayed, all the things that are usually done before one buys a horse. But, I had conferred with Hawk Eye, and Hawk Eye gave her the okay, which was good enough for me. He was watching over us, I knew it. Savannah would come to my barn the end of that week, and I already felt like I'd known her a long time. I'd been preparing, and feeling better than I'd felt since I lost Hawk Eye. So I guess that Savannah rescued me as much as I rescued her, and now it doesn't seem trite at all.

It's now been exactly a month since Savannah Belle cautiously, but with presence, walked off the horse trailer into the aisle of Centerline Stables. Immediately her curiosity, innocence, and courage were evident. Obviously, her life experiences had served her well and she was a survivor. I was really choked up watching her slowly find her way to her stall. All my anxieties were close to the surface: Would she love me like I already loved her? Would she be ready to learn what she needed to know to be my companion? Would she be healthy and happy in her new home?

Well, the news is great! The following morning, after Savannah had spent her first night ever indoors, she allowed herself to be groomed and haltered. In fact she seemed to love the attention and the brushing. Her personality began to emerge as sweet, very loving and affectionate, brave, curious, sensible, and

> She is adorable, sassy, and smart. I can see that already, and I can't wait to be a part of her life.

I already feel like I've known her for a long time.

grounded. Her entire world had been turned upside down, for the better of course, but still it must have been disconcerting to her. Within the next day or two, she was seen by the vet, the farrier, and the nutritionist. With each one, she was cooperative and behaved almost as if she knew that all were there to help her transition into her new world. In the last few weeks, she has been vacuumed, has gone into the wash stalls, has been led to different paddocks, and has even taken a stroll into the indoor arena.

All of this is amazing to say the least, but for me the most amazing part is how I feel like I have known her all my life. I can't wait to get up each day to see, feel, and smell her again. And her response to me makes it so worthwhile. I literally melt when I rub her ears and she pushes her head into me as if to say, "That's the spot!" And when she is a bit worried, she seems to look to me as part of her "herd." She loves to run and play and buck during turnout, and has a joyous headshake, mane flowing as she scampers around, to express that it's good to be alive.

I just couldn't be happier. I smile when I think of her, see her, and touch her. If for some reason I never even get to ride her, it will be okay. It is like having a new best friend.

Continuing Aspirations—Café Mocha

DONNA CLOUTIER AND BRIANA CLOUTIER

It was a typically cool November morning, the year 2004, and I was on my way to meet and photograph the new PMU foals that had just arrived from Canada only two days prior. On this particular day I was also accompanied by my husband, Norm, who, much like myself, has also enjoyed horses in his life.

We arrived at the farm in Albany, New York, where the foals were settling in, each waiting to embark on the next step of his or her individual journey. There were approximately thirty foals varying in size, color, breed, and personality. My mission on this day was to photograph each foal as well as photograph the group to document their progress along this step of the adoption process. These photos would then be placed on the EARS website, where potential adopters could get a first glance of their soon-to-be new family member.

As I engrossed myself with the task at hand, my concentration was quietly dispelled by the soft-spoken, unexpected words of my husband: "How about we take another one home?" Calling my reaction "shocked" would be no less than a blatant understatement, considering Norm had not even blinked in the direction of another horse since the passing of his beloved Quarter Horse, Dynamite, one January morning five years earlier. I knew that the little filly, foal number 33, that had caught his eye must truly

Mocha at six months old plays in the first snow in her new home.

be something special. Knowing my husband, this was a moment to be seized as his rationality would soon set in and he would immediately fall back on his frequent claim that "we already have to many animals."

I quietly pulled Frank Weller aside to find out all that I could about the little Clydesdale filly shyly hovering just outside the herd. He told me that she was one that we needed to pull from the larger group and place in foster care until finding her forever home so that she could

Norm and Mocha are a perfect team!

Mocha enjoys a good roll . . .

. . . and rest in the snow.

thrive without the challenges of living among a herd. I knew right then and there that we were to be her "forever home." Now I just had to convince Norm.

Within the following week foal number 33 had arrived at a foster home in Roxbury, Connecticut, only minutes from our farm. As predicted, Norm had convinced himself that we really didn't need another horse and we didn't have an available stall in the barn anyway. The kids and I visited the filly often and reported her progress to Norm weekly. We provided details about her lovely disposition and remarkable personality. Finally Norm's heart outweighed his rational thinking, and on Christmas Eve 2004 Café Mocha finally arrived home.

Within the first weeks we knew we had a very special girl. During that first year we visited Girl Scout troops and participated in fund-raisers and celebrations to raise awareness of the PMU foals. She even stood quietly, happily greeting passersby on a street corner of Fifth Avenue in New

Donna rides Mocha for the first time at Rolling M Ranch, Southbury, Connecticut. PHOTO COURTESY OF ROCCO VALERI

159

Her willing personality and calm nature make her a pleasure to be with.

PHOTOS COURTESY OF KIERA LEE CLOUTIER

York City for four hours with rescue organization volunteers in an effort to raise awareness and show firsthand just how magnificent these PMU horses are.

She spent her second year mostly at the farm, playing with her stable mates as well as learning her basic ground skills. We spent time trick training as a way to build our relationship and our ongoing trust of one another. As a three-year-old she spent three months with horse trainer Joe McAllister of Rolling M Ranch in Southbury, Connecticut. Her willing personality and calm nature made her

We (Donna and Mocha) have completed two hunter paces . . .

. . . and have taken pleasure trail rides through the woods, as well as continued ring work. PHOTO COURTESY OF ROCCO VALERI

an excellent student. She has since continued to grow and learn new skills. We have completed two hunter paces and have taken pleasure trail rides through the woods, as well as continued ring work. Norm has even begun to ride again, having a wonderful new mount. Our continued aspirations for her include possible carriage or sleigh driving, English and western pleasure riding, as well as advancing her trick training, if only to keep her sharp and playful mind occupied. We look forward to all the possibilities that she has before her knowing that she can and will try anything.

Forty Foals 'Til Dustin

The Beginning—Leslie Legan

Frank Weller called me about saving forty foals in Manitoba, Canada, from going to a slaughter auction. He said that he could cover the transport if I could pay for the foals. I knew a lot about the plight and about their certain fate if he could not help them and so I volunteered to help save them. The trip was long, but I went directly to see the foals and, upon arriving, what I saw took my breath away. Dozens of foals, in chestnut, bay, and paint, were wandering around. Some were walking, some were trotting, but all of them seemed to be in a state of depression.

It was then that I noticed one particular colt. He was much smaller than the other four-month-old foals, maybe because he was born in June instead of May. He was a mixture of Thoroughbred and Quarter Horse, a dark bay. This little fellow was all legs, and despite his poor condition, I could still see he had a spirited personality. He simply didn't realize that he was smaller than the rest. As the foals continued to run along the fence rails, he struggled to keep up with the herd. Although he was rather weak and scrawny, I noticed his inner strength and determination. There was something extraordinary about his conformation and his movement that told me that he could become very beautiful.

The little colt had his head down and his tail to the side, a sign he wasn't well. The old farmer realized that all the rescues would be turned

The little colt had his head down and his tail to the side, a sign he wasn't feeling well. PHOTO COURTESY OF LESLIE LEGAN

back at the border if one was sick, and so he gave the little guy some penicillin and shaved the number 26 on his side. He was on his way to the USA.

Frank found a temporary foster home for number 26 at a nice place that was adjacent to Dustin Hoffman's house in Connecticut. I am a big fan of Hoffman, and so naturally number 26 became Dustin. Although he never met his namesake, Frank introduced Baby Dustin to Za Manocherian and Sara Vanecek from Centerline Stables. They also saw the spark in him and took him on. Upon delivery, Dustin got off the trailer, took a look around and, with his friend Chico, started his journey to find the depth of his potential. So many people helped polish this diamond in the rough, by caring, training, and covering expenses. We are all so proud and so fortunate to have been able to help him and watch him, and many others, blossom and spread their wings!

DUSTIN FINDS SANCTUARY AT CENTERLINE STABLES—OLIVIA MARTIN

Performance Feeding adopted and started working with Dustin in February of 2005. What we found at Centerline Stables that February was a scrawny youngster who was just learning how to interact with people and adapt to a new environment.

Dustin's first hurdle was just getting well enough to start on the way to better health; a round of deworming was prescribed by Centerline's veterinarian. With that out of the way, slow progress was made on the way to helping Dustin gain some weight and acclimate to his new life.

By March of 2005, it was clear that Dustin had turned a corner and was going to be a stunning youngster. Time out on pasture and constant handling by the Centerline staff made Dustin a cheery and playful young colt. However, Dustin's biggest hurdle lay ahead. It was clear by the end of March 2005 that Dustin suffered from a form of angular limb deformity in both front legs. As a result of a lack of adequate nutrition from the time Dustin was still in his mother's womb, the tendons in his front legs became contracted, worse in the front right than the left. The condition did not inhibit Dustin's movement, and he continued to be a sound and active young horse.

However, without careful attention to Dustin's nutrition, the situation could turn from a mild case into a totally debilitating condition. The challenge at this stage was to deliver just enough calories to encourage normal growth without causing sudden growth spurts, which may cause the condition to worsen.

We encouraged as much time outside as possible for Dustin to move around and to help his legs to straighten. Dustin's team of caregivers

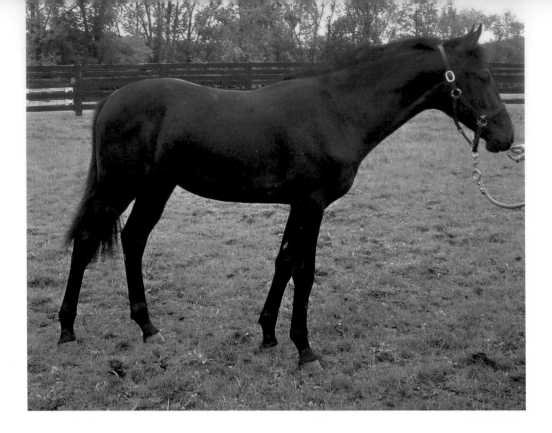

By March 2006, Dustin was almost two and had transformed from a scrawny, tentative weanling into a maturing, handsome, and very friendly young horse. PHOTO COURTESY OF OLIVIA MARTIN

carefully monitored his calories and vigilantly watched his legs. Around this time, the Centerline trainers started Dustin playfully "working" with ground aids and desensitivity-type obstacle courses. Dustin proved to be a willing partner and was a star every time out.

By March of 2006, Dustin was a few months short of turning two and had transformed from a scrawny, tentative weanling into a maturing, handsome, and very friendly young horse. Even though Dustin still had some growing to do, by moderating his diet and watching his growth carefully, we were able to prevent a serious case of limb dysfunction from becoming a chronic problem.

Toward the end of 2007, Dustin's legs, although not perfect, were straight enough and sound enough to give Dustin a chance at becoming a valued riding partner for students at the Ethel Walker School in Simsbury, Connecticut.

DUSTIN BLOSSOMS AT ETHEL WALKER SCHOOL—McKENZIE ROLLINS

Dustin is an old soul. You can see it in his eyes. He is so willing to learn, and to try anything that lies ahead of him. I suppose that is why he is so grateful for every opportunity he is given. Here at Ethel Walker, he is "Baby Dusty" to the many girls who roam the barn aisles. They are all in love with him. They squeal in delight when he enters the ring, they speak adoringly to him as he nickers when they walk past, and he stands patiently and lovingly as they hang off of him, bombarding him with hugs and kisses. In relation to all the big jumping horses, Dustin, like his namesake, is small in stature, but big in spirit.

Just recently Baby Dusty was in the annual holiday ride. Under dim lights he paraded around the hundred-foot

Dustin is an old soul.

Christmas tree that stood in the center of the indoor ring, with holiday music blasting from the sound system and decorations glimmering in the festive lighting. Baby Dusty was the leader of the Middle School Hanukah Drill ride. Eleven older horses followed the youngest and bravest into the darkened arena. Dressed smartly in a fresh white saddle pad, with matching white polo wraps, he marched around proudly, showing off for the crowd of parents and children packed shoulder to shoulder in the viewing gallery. Dustin exemplified poise, bravery, and honesty not often found in young horses. He has certainly become an asset to our program and is always an enthusiastic student himself. Often the center of attention, Dustin has settled into his role here at Ethel Walker quite comfortably, and it is safe to say that everyone who has ever met this little horse from Canada is truly honored.

EPILOGUE

Horses teach us a lot about life and, all too often, much about death as well. Speeding down the Massachusetts Turnpike during a winter snowfall, I sat on the floor of a stock trailer with the head of a nine-month-old foal in my lap. Anna, the driver, was zooming past eighteen-wheel trucks that would angrily downshift as our small rig shot by. A stock trailer characteristically has slotted open upper walls, and so falling snow gently wafted in as the early morning's grayish light bounced off of it.

The life in my lap was slowly slipping away as we raced toward Tufts Large Animal Hospital, trying to save her. It had been a hard night, too cruel and too cold to recount, but Laurie, the foal, put up a brave fight. I'll never forget when she looked up at me with her soft brown eyes and drew her last breath. I wasn't even sure if she had passed away at that moment, but within seconds that seemed much longer, I could tell. I knew that we were very close to Tufts, and so I tried CPR for about fifteen minutes before the cold reality set in. The spirituality of the moment and the utter exhaustion both hit me at once. It was horribly sad and strangely peaceful at the same time. A silent snowstorm fell inside the speeding trailer as I tried to make sense of Laurie's passing. A sense of loss overwhelmed me while I lay next to her and tried to let her go. I was tired and it was hard to think that she was on her way to a better place.

It is not just in death that we can learn about letting go. There is a similar lesson for me when a horse we've bonded with is adopted and then delivered to a new home. I had a hard time when I brought an eighteen-month-old Belgian filly to her new family only twelve rugged miles away. Her name was Zoey and she had been with me for over a year. It seemed to put a hole in my life when she left. I had fed her morning and night, checked her before bed, greeted her several times a day, bathed her, and frequently walked her for training. Zoey was the only young rescued horse on the farm and she captivated every heart she met. I knew that she was going to her forever adoption home and that I had to make room for other rescues, but the sadness of her loss took my breath away for a long time. Someday we must say goodbye to all we love, and letting go on any level is difficult. Life, of course, is a lesson in letting go, as it is full of change. It is so much easier for me if I can think of the bigger picture and realize that it is necessary to let go and let God take care of things so that I can move on in my spiritual journey as others do the same.

I have often thought of it in a different way. Many times I must move horses. They usually have buddies and maybe they are grazing together on a sparkling day in a lush green field. I pull up with my trailer and take one of them away to his new loving and lifelong home. That horse has graduated and been adopted into a wonderful family that will love him dearly. The horses left behind, however, don't know that and all they see is that their buddy has left. In their minds, he is gone and they may race along the fence line calling to him and missing him. But his friends don't know about the new and better life that horse has found. I like to think of death as that kind of graduation, and I can actually be comfortable with letting go when looking at that bigger picture. In all cases, however, I did not deny myself the process of grieving. I deeply experienced that feeling of loss and sadness and it takes each of us a different amount of time to process and move through it. I say "move through" grief, because I don't think that I ever get over it. I know that I will always miss Laurie and Zoey as if they were my everyday buddies grazing in a sun-soaked field, but I keep moving as I grieve, because I know that other horses need me and there is much work to be done.

We never give up before the miracles of peace, joy, and love.

Horses can teach us much about life and death, but mostly they teach us about ourselves. If we're open to the lessons, they can transport

us a long way on our life's spiritual journey and beyond. We at EARS have been blessed to have had over 250 highly energetic teachers, and they each have given us new lessons with different teaching methods. We have learned never to give up as we are working, training, or fighting for the horses, and we never quit before the miracle of a breakthrough. The birth, rescue, sanctuary, and blossoming of these God-given equines has been a joyous honor to touch and to be touched by.

I often find solace and peace while visiting with the horses. On my most recent visit, looking for inspiration, I was awed by the golden clouds of sunset, ablaze with electric peach-colored bellies, turning to shimmering tangerine. Their wispy edges were cradled by the crisp turquoise sky. Dark silvery grey clouds sailed by serenely in search of the next rain storm that they might care to create.

The sun was pleasantly setting, but there had been days of constant rain. It was too late in the day for a normal rainbow, but the spectrum of brilliant yellow and gold tones played upon the bottoms of these previously punishing clouds. Maybe not a covenant with God, I thought, but certainly a truce. I can only hope that while the sun sets on the PMU industry, we also have a truce for the horses until the next abusive behavior from mankind comes along. We can shine our golden light upon the dismal problems and maybe good people will come sooner to the rescue. It is good to be with the horses and with the light of sunset after a dark day. I pray that a better day will dawn as I see many rescued by the light they shine in the graceful act of rescue.

As the day closes into the night, the stars are coming out to light the darkening sky. The horses feel at home under the endless sky and they once again reassure me, because they are calming. We can make a difference to each horse we touch. They in turn light our world and give us hope that sometimes the world can be loving and kind. Thank you for being stars and angels. As always, for the horses, and from them too, we wish you peace, joy, and love.

ACKNOWLEDGMENTS

I could not compile a complete list of all the adopters, foster families, donors, volunteers—people who have helped us, taught us, and inspired us over the last seven years. I know that many praises will go unsung. A new book could be written, as their stories are also rich in rescue, rewards, and challenges.

There are three mentors in the equine world who have given me great insight into the plight of the foals, their rescue, and the big picture. The examples of their tireless dedication have inspired me and many others. Dr. Ray Kellosami has done incredible work on behalf of and with the horses. As an OB/GYN he has successfully taken hundreds of his patients off of Premarin, and I don't know of any who have returned to it. He has spread that awareness beyond his colleagues, beyond Canada, and to anyone in the world who is concerned enough to listen. Dr. Ray enlightens us with his expertise and has led with skill, connection, and brilliance. Humans and equines benefit from the passion he has devoted to the horses who are at risk for slaughter. Words cannot thank him enough.

Dr. Kellosami's sister, Sinikka Crosland, is another dedicated fighter for the foals, mares, and other animals. She has often helped us at Equine Angels Rescue Sanctuary, although we have yet to meet her. We are not only inspired by all that she does with The Responsible Animal Care Society (TRACS), her agency in Canada, but by the way that she does it. She is angelic in her nature, creative in her advocacy, and happily helps our horse rescue efforts. The Premarin Foal Rescue Caravan, a national effort to put a face on the innocent foals who have been tragically slaughtered, would not have happened without her tapping away on the Internet with her computer keyboard. Sinikka gets good things done.

The lead mare disciplines the herd.

Lastly, but equally, we are all inspired by Helen Meredith. Her knowledge of horses, especially foals, is amazing. Helen's diverse background—from being a jockey, to training champion thoroughbreds, and then to rescuing them—has prepared her for leadership in the rescuing of mares, foals, and stallions, too. She founded United Pegasus, which is the model on the west coast for what EARS does on the east coast. Totally immersed in the rescue challenge, she has put many horses and humans on that path. After witnessing her work ethic, we aspire to do a fraction of what she does!

I can only reiterate that all of these mentors have superhuman dedication and skill. These few paragraphs are a scant thank you, but then the rescued equines say it best, and that is heartwarming. They say thank you in their safety and with the joy they bring to many people. And the horses also say thank you for caring rescue teamwork by giving back to all who love enough to help.

There are two other rescue mentors that I will never forget. Their credentials are not with horses, but with people. They are Bob McCauley and his wife Leila, who founded AmeriCares. I frequently take a page from their success story and apply it to horse rescue. I have been honored to travel with and represent the relief efforts of AmeriCares in other countries, including Albania, Honduras, and even North Korea. By documenting their humanitarian work, I learned about the world, myself, and effective rescue strategies. Bob and Leila taught me what selfless love means to others, how to help, and how to beg. All elements, especially the latter, are necessary for success in saving horses. Bob and Leila are heroes of mine, they are definitely angels, and I am proud to be a minor ripple in their humanitarian wake.

As for writing the book, however, I first thank God for letting me be here (thanks for getting me this far and please help me make it the rest of the way) and my mother, Fran, and late father, Don, for getting me here in so many other ways. My late stepfather Bob also fostered my growth. My sister Emmy along with Mike, and brother Vann and his family Lucinda, Drew, and Laura Marie, have been there for the long ride. My daughters Ali, recently wed to Connor, and Caitlyn, who typed and formatted furiously, and their mom Lise have all been blessings to me throughout the many miles of this marathon. (I promised Cait a whole chapter, but maybe in the next book.)

Other organizations, barns, and individuals have been incredibly helpful to the rescue. The wonderful staff at Centerline Stables not only went the extra miles, but they did it with smiles. Especially the smiles and TLC from Za and Donald Manocherian, Sara Vanecek, and Nancy Goldmark. Anna Twinney, a wonderful trainer, teacher, and friend, always reached out to us and to all the horses. In Afton, New York, Anne Flaherty and Phil Scribner spend every waking moment with the horses and most sleeping moments, too. Carl Dunham and Nancy Saggese have given the foals and mares safety and security at Candlelight Farm in Connecticut and at Berkshire Equestrian in Massachusetts. Leslie Legan undertook many journeys of caring, financing, and driving for the mares and foals. Terri Plunkett and her parents, Bill and Joan, hosted hundreds of foals and many mares along their rescue journey. Rob and Tiffany DeMartin of Thunder Ridge Farm (see their story, Leap of Faith), together with daughters Augusta and Penelope, housed horses, shared friendship and dreams, and always pitched in to do whatever was needed. Leslie Ballotti and her family (see her story, Plan A) have carried the torch for five Premarin horses at a difficult time for three of the older mares. Brooke Baxter, who helped develop this book, shared vision and advice, and is a vigorous advocate for the mares and foals. Elaine Shields deserves thanks for the first and best horse lessons that enlivened my passion, insight, and connection with equine souls. Mia Genovese at God's Speed Horse Hostel in Amenia, New York, now has five of our foals

Savannah has rescued me as much as I have rescued her.

trained and looking grand; what a saint! She has also saved two slaughter-bound mares. A special thank you to angels Peter and Mary Gregory, founders of "The Retirement Home for Horses" in Alachua, Florida, who by putting their heart, soul, and total retirement savings into saving aged horses have deeply inspired us and many others. Lastly, chronologically, but certainly not least, thanks to Bonnie, Eve, and the caring people at Ray of Light Farm in East Haddam, Connecticut. All of them share the vision of rescue, but also went the extra miles to transport, train, and protect the foals and mares of the 2008 rescue. A hearty thank you to all those who rescue and therefore made the book possible, from all of us at Equine Angels Rescue Sanctuary. You are all angelic voluntEARS and a blessing to the equines and people who meet you.

A special thanks to all of the writers who shared their stories within this book. Your stories will soar to great heights in helping horses find their homes. Thank you to Maureen Graney, my interim editor, whose gentle and respectful care made it possible to spread my wings on this first flight, and Kathryn Mennone who first saw the potential for The Lyons Press in this adventure. Thanks also to Lilly Golden and Jane Wise, who also inspired me along the way. Thank you to Erin Turner, a valued editor, who I haven't met yet, but who has gracefully added polish to this book. Also, thank you to the many artistic hands whom I probably will not meet that touch this book along the way, including designers, printers, promoters, and people whose jobs I am not even aware of. Ellen Urban and Jessie Shiers are shining among them. Thank you all for helping the horses by telling their story.

Thank you especially to Donna Cloutier for lending her time and talent and for helping develop the vision for this book. Her amazing photography conveys the spirit and connection with the horses, and her donations to the rescue have benefited all of the equines. Her husband Norm and her family also deserve thanks for parting with her so often, as do mine. I certainly believe that we have all received rescue blessings.

Finally, I humbly thank you, the reader, for caring enough to pick up this book and entering it on any level. Whether you find value in it now, later, or seemingly never at all, I believe that in some way, it has changed your life. Your life will change others and the ripples will continue. Thank you for diving in.

ABOUT THE AUTHOR

Frank Weller is a graduate of Boston University with a degree in film, broadcast journalism, and communications. He was a partner in a successful retail store while working to document the relief efforts of AmeriCares at home and throughout the world.

He was also helpful in establishing an AmeriCares medical clinic for the under-insured and uninsured in Danbury, Connecticut. Frank produced an award-winning community television show with his daughters for three years and then founded a film commission to bring film projects to the town of New Milford, Connecticut. He serves and has served in many community agencies and has been working as a location scout for film companies and rescuing horses for the last eight years. He currently lives on a farm in New Milford, Connecticut.

ABOUT THE PHOTOGRAPHER

Donna M. Cloutier is a professional freelance photographer, as well as an active member of a local photography club, in which she enjoys the fellowship and inspiration to grow in the art of photography. She uses her talent and passion not only for her own art, but also as a mentor for young minds in her community, to help them sharpen their own creative views and abilities. Many of her images have placed in local and regional competitions as well as some published work. She also is the originator of Just Another Nif-T Greeting and Nif-T Creations, in which she designs greeting cards and custom fine art prints.

Donna lives on a small farm in Connecticut with her husband, their three daughters, and a variety of animals, large and small, many of them rescues. To learn more about Donna and her work you can find her on the web at www.shezanifty.com.

ABOUT EQUINE ANGELS RESCUE SANCTUARY

The Equine Angels Rescue Sanctuary was established as a 501(c)3, non-profit agency. Its goal is to rescue foals, mares, geldings, and stallions and place them into loving homes. We rescue the equines from slaughter and qualify potential adopters and foster homes. We do site inspections and monitor progress of new "families" with follow-up visits and/or veterinarian reports.

We believe that we are responsible to both parties for the success of the new relationship.